D0772497

Butterflies

by Mari C. Schuh

Consulting Editor: Gail Saunders-Smith, Ph.D.

Consultant: Gary A. Dunn, Director of Education,
Young Entomologists' Society

Pebble Books

an imprint of Capstone Press
Mankato, Minnesota

Pebble Books are published by Capstone Press
151 Good Counsel Drive, P.O. Box 669, Mankato, Minnesota 56002
http://www.capstone-press.com

1 2 3 4 5 6 08 07 06 05 04 03

Library of Congress Cataloging-in-Publication Data
Schuh, Mari C., 1975–
    Butterflies / by Mari C. Schuh.
    p. cm.—(Insects)
    Summary: Simple text and photographs present the features and behavior
of butterflies.
    Includes bibliographical references (p. 23) and index.
    ISBN 0-7368-1664-X (hardcover)
    1. Butterflies—Juvenile literature. [1. Butterflies.] I. Title. II. Insects (Mankato,
Minn.)
QL544.2 .S38 2003
595.78'9—dc21   2002010398

Note to Parents and Teachers

The Insects series supports national science standards for units on the diversity and unity of life. The series shows that insects have features that help them live in different environments. This book describes and illustrates butterflies and their parts and habits. The photographs support early readers in understanding the text. The repetition of words and phrases helps early readers learn new words. This book also introduces early readers to subject-specific vocabulary words, which are defined in the Words to Know section. Early readers may need assistance to read some words and to use the Table of Contents, Words to Know, Read More, Internet Sites, and Index/Word List sections of the book.

Table of Contents

Body 5
Wings 15
Where Butterflies Live 19

Words to Know 22
Read More 23
Internet Sites 23
Index/Word List 24

wings

wings

Butterflies have
four wings.

6

Butterflies have
thin bodies.

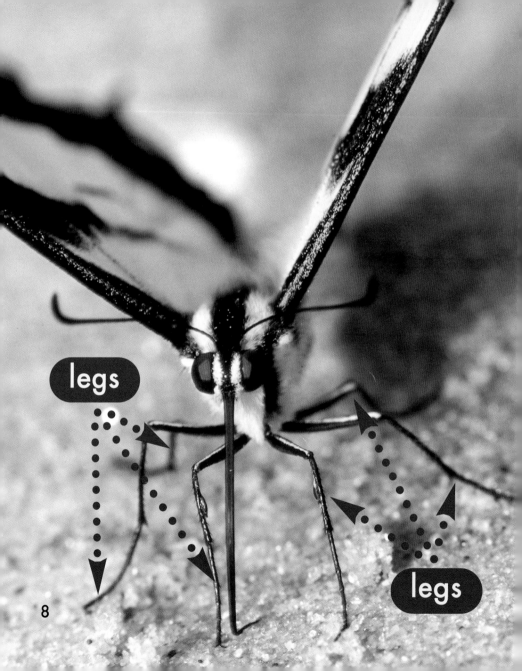

legs

legs

8

Butterflies have
six legs.

antennas

Butterflies have
two thin antennas.

proboscis

Butterflies have
a proboscis.

Butterfly wings
have tiny scales.

Butterfly wings
have colorful patterns.

Most butterflies live
near plants and flowers.

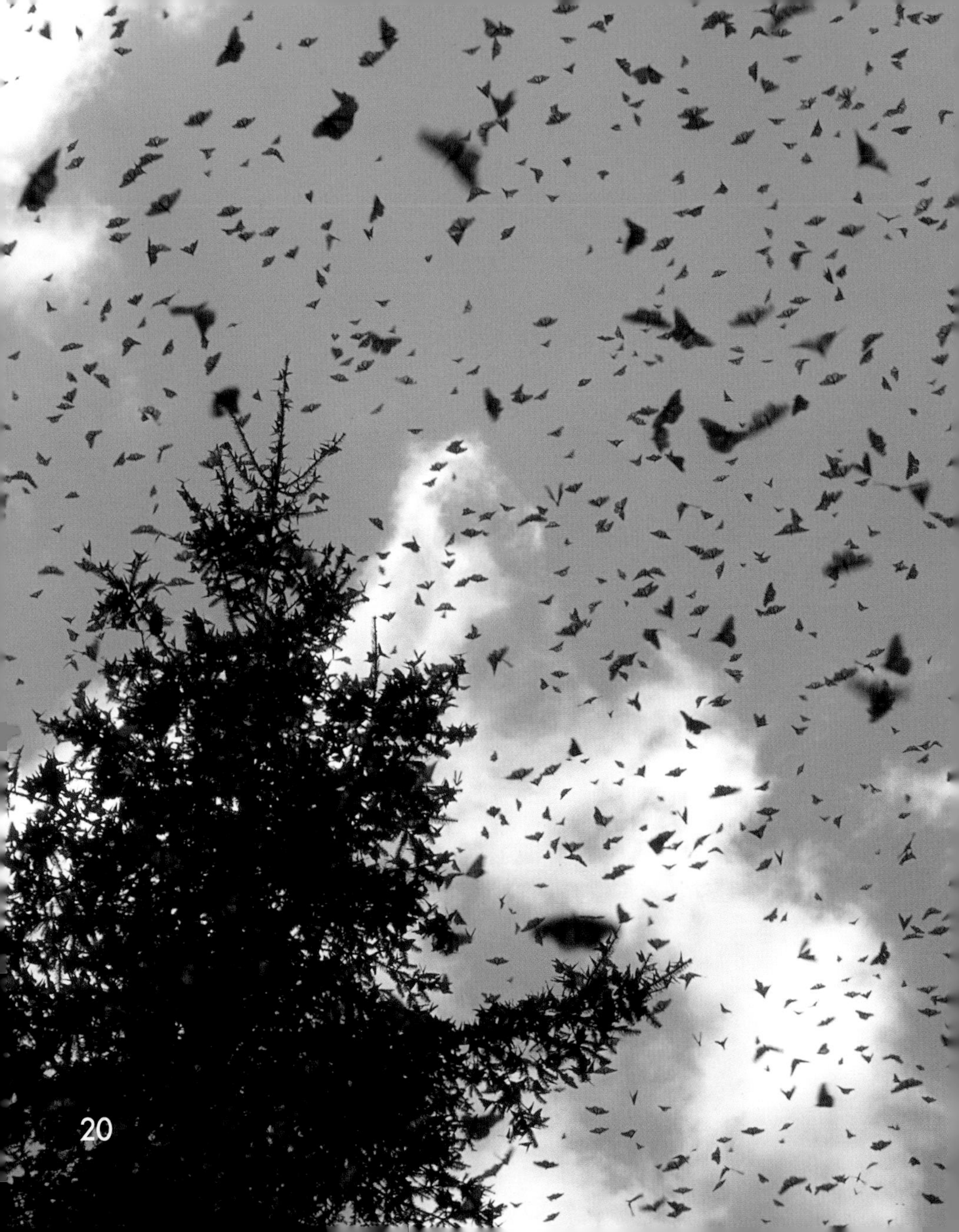

Some butterflies migrate
to warm places
in the winter.

Words to Know

antenna—a feeler on an insect's head; butterflies use antennas to smell.

migrate—to go away at a certain time of year to live in another place; some butterflies migrate south during the fall and north during the spring.

pattern—a repeated set of colors and shapes; patterns help butterflies communicate with each other, warn predators, and hide.

proboscis—a long, tube-shaped mouthpart

scales—small pieces of hard skin that cover the wings of a butterfly; each scale is smaller than a grain of sand.

wing—the movable part of a butterfly that helps it fly

Read More

Frost, Helen. *Butterfly Colors.* Butterflies. Mankato, Minn.: Pebble Books, 1999.

Hovanec, Erin M. *I Wonder What It's Like to Be a Butterfly.* A Life Science Wonder Book. New York: PowerKids Press, 2000.

Murray, Julie. *Butterflies.* Animal Kingdom. Edina, Minn.: Abdo Publishing, 2002.

Internet Sites

Track down many sites about butterflies. Visit the FACT HOUND at *http://www.facthound.com*

IT IS EASY! IT IS FUN!

1) Go to *http://www.facthound.com*

2) Type in: 073681664X

3) Click on "FETCH IT" and FACT HOUND will find several links hand-picked by our editors.

Relax and let our pal FACT HOUND do the research for you!

Index/Word List

antennas, 11

bodies, 7

colorful, 17

flowers, 19

four, 5

legs, 9

live, 19

migrate, 21

most, 19

near, 19

patterns, 17

places, 21

plants, 19

proboscis, 13

scales, 15

six, 9

some, 21

thin, 7, 11

tiny, 15

two, 11

warm, 21

wings, 5, 15, 17

winter, 21

Word Count: 47
Early-Intervention Level: 8

Editorial Credits

Hollie J. Endres, editor; Timothy Halldin, cover designer and illustrator; Molly Nei, designer; Karrey Tweten, photo researcher

Photo Credits

Bill Johnson, 12

Bruce Coleman Inc./Bob Jensen, cover; Bob Gossington, 1; Roger Wilmshurst, 4

Photovault.com/Wernher Krutein, 16

Richard Cummins, 6

Visuals Unlimited/Jonathan Speer, 8; Bill Kamin, 10; Kjell B. Sandved, 14; Gary W. Carter, 18; Fritz Polking, 20

The author dedicates this book to her friend, Liz Grotte of Fairmont, Minnesota.